D1444799

The Story of EASTER

The Story of EASTER

Jesus Enters Jerusalem
The Bread and the Wine
Good Friday • Happy Easter

An **ARCH BOOKS**® Gift Collection

An Inspirational Press Book
for Children

First Inspirational Press edition published in 1998.

Inspirational Press
A division of BBS Publishing Corporation
386 Park Avenue South
New York, NY 10016

Inspirational Press is a registered trademark of BBS Publishing Corporation.

Published by arrangement with ARCH® Books, a division of Concordia
Publishing House, 3558 S. Jefferson Ave., St. Louis, MO 63118-3968.

Library of Congress Catalog Card Number: 97-77417
ISBN: 0-88486-200-3

Printed in Mexico.

Jesus Enters Jerusalem

Matthew 21:1–11
Mark 11:1–11
Luke 19:28–38
John 12:12–19 for children

Written by Jane L. Fryar
Illustrated by Michelle Dorenkamp

In spring of each and every year,
God's people came from far and near
To tell what their great God had done,
To shout the victory He had won.

"Let's go up for the feast," they said.
"Let's hear the ancient story read.
Let's praise our Lord who set us free
From Pharaoh and from slavery."

"You've saved us, God!" the people sang.
Along the road their glad song rang.
"Hosanna! Save us once again!
Hosanna! Save! Amen! Amen!"

As Jesus neared the city gate,
He paused and asked His friends to wait.
He looked at them, then said to two,
"I have a job for you . . . and you.

"Go to the village over there.
Look for two donkeys—colt and mare.
Untie them. Bring them here to Me.
I need them, as you soon will see.

"If someone tries to stop you, say,
'The Master sent us here today.
He needs the colt. Please, let us do
What our Lord Jesus told us to.'"

So off the two disciples sped,
Found everything as Jesus said,
Untied the donkeys, walked away.
And then a voice rang out: "Wait! Hey!

"What is it that you people think?
Why, next you'll take my kitchen sink!
What other plans have you right now?
To steal my goat? My lamb? Or cow?"

But Jesus' friends knew what to say:
"The Master sent us here today.
He needs the colt. Please let us do
What our Lord Jesus told us to."

The donkeys' owner nodded. Then,
He sent the colt with Jesus' men.
They hurried back up toward the road
To find the Lord, as they'd been told.

The first time someone rides a colt,
It often tries to buck or bolt.
But this colt let the Lord sit down
Upon its back without a frown.

The little donkey walked along
Into the city while the song
That told of God's great love rang out,
And Jesus heard the people shout.

"Hosanna, Jesus! You're our King!
Hosanna! Save! To You we sing!
Hosanna! Praise! We shout again.
Hosanna! Praise! Amen! Amen!"

Then someone cut a palm branch flag.
And someone else began to drag
His outer cloak upon the street,
Right under Jesus' donkey's feet.

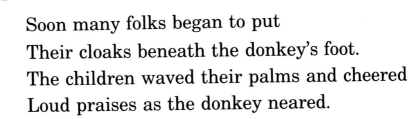

Soon many folks began to put
Their cloaks beneath the donkey's foot.
The children waved their palms and cheered
Loud praises as the donkey neared.

The Savior knew that this glad song
Would turn to hate before too long.
He knew what He in love would do
To save all people—me and you.

He saw the cross. He knew that there
Our loneliness and pain He'd bear.
Still on He rode to death and grave
And resurrection. On to save!

"You've saved us, Lord! today we sing.
Hosanna! You're the Lord, our King!
Hosanna! Praise! we shout again.
Hosanna! Praise! Amen! Amen!"

Dear Parents:

The crowds that came to Jerusalem to celebrate the Passover during the third year of Jesus' earthly ministry cheered Him as their King, their deliverer. "Hosanna! Save us, Lord!" they shouted. Five short days later, a mob, perhaps made up of many of the same people, roared, "Away with this man! Crucify Him!"

The crowd didn't understand Jesus. They didn't want the kind of king that God the Father had planned for them. They wanted freedom from life under the Roman army's boot. Jesus came to free them from Satan's power. They wanted deliverance from Roman occupation and taxation. Jesus came to deliver them from sin and the fear of death.

Though many people today still reject Jesus and His kingdom, He continues to offer us life in that kingdom, as well as forgiveness, freedom, joy, and peace. As you read and talk with your child about the day many Christians call Palm Sunday, celebrate the new life Jesus has given you.

The Editor

THE BREAD AND THE WINE

The Story of the Last Supper

**The Last Supper, John 13:1-38,
1 Corinthians 11:23-34 FOR CHILDREN**

Written by Denise Ahern
Illustrated by Alice Hausner

Ben loved to play in his large house
a game of hide and seek.
He had a special, secret place
where he alone could peek.

A tiny closet, dark and snug,
    where jars and bowls were stored,
was where he'd sit; his eyes shone bright
    through a crack in the closet door.

One day he heard his mother say
that guests would soon arrive,
so up the stairs he rapidly raced
and hid where he could spy.

Two men walked in, their arms heaped high
    with baskets, jars, and bowls.
They set the table, then neatly placed
    bright pillows in two rows.

A delicious smell filled the room,
    of roasted lamb and bread;
in walked Ben's mother with the food.
    "We're ready to dine," they said.

On the stairs Ben heard footsteps;
a crowd of friends came in.
Around the table each took his place;
Ben counted 13 men.

They started then to sing a song;
    the man in the center beamed—
But one man wore a tight-lipped frown.
    Ben thought, "He sure looks mean."

The leader rose, He tucked His robe,
poured water from a vase,
and set the bowl upon the floor.

A smile played on His face.
Then like a servant He dipped a towel
and went down to His knees.

"That's Jesus," Ben stared in surprise,
   "I heard the people sing
that day when He rode through the streets
   'Hosannah to the King!'

"If He is King, He should not wash
their feet, that's servant's work."
Jesus explained, "As I have done,
each other you must serve."

Then Jesus sat and prayed, "Dear God,
please bless this Passover meal."
They feasted on the lamb and bread,
began to eat their fill.

Ben thought of Passover, the very first—
   God's people, the Jews, each chose
a lamb with wool so soft and white,
   the one they loved the most.

They spread its blood upon their door
so God would keep them safe
and lead them from the land of Egypt
where they worked hard as slaves.

Jesus was silent; tears filled His eyes.
Ben thought, "He looks so sad."
His friends whispered, "What is wrong?
Let's try to make Him glad."

They thought of the past and Peter said,
    "Remember that time at sea?
I walked to meet You on the water
    but sank up to my knees!"
Jesus smiled—a tender smile,
    "You've learned a lot since then."
"They love Jesus so much," Ben thought
    "They really are good friends."

Ben listened; Jesus softly spoke,
 "My betrayer is here this night."
Wonderingly, the 12 men stared;
 each asked, "Lord, is it I?"

Beside Jesus sat one man;
    his eyes were wide with fear.
Trembling he whispered, "Is it I?"
    Ben strained hard to hear.

A man named John leaned toward Jesus,
"Who is it, Lord?" he said.
Jesus slowly turned and gave
the frightened man His bread.

"Judas, go," then Jesus spoke,
　　"and do what must be done."
With scowling brow, Judas fled;
　　Ben said, "I'm glad he's gone!"

Jesus sighed a deep, long sigh;
His face was very grave.
He broke in half a loaf of bread
and bowed His head to pray.

"Take and eat; this is My body,
given for your sins."
Jesus passed the bread around
to each one of His friends.

Ben thought, "The other day I tied
a rock to my cat's tail;
she spun around, jumped on the table—
then crash—a clay pot fell!

My mother says that it is sin
when I do what is bad.
All the men seem so unhappy;
for sin makes Jesus sad."

Then Jesus took a cup of wine.

Ben thought, "What will He do?"

Jesus said, "This is God's new covenant
sealed with My blood, shed for you.

Do this to remember Me.

Drink this cup of Mine."

Ben watched as each man raised the cup
and tasted the sweet wine.

All the men joined in to sing
a song in closing prayer.
Their voices rang in highest praise
that burst the still night air.

Quietly they left the room;
Ben heard their footsteps echo
on the stairs and through the streets
as after Him they followed.

Ben sat alone; the room was dark;
    but he was not afraid.
He still could see the gentle eyes,
    the smile on Jesus' face.

Scooting from his hiding place,
he felt so stiff and sore.
He quickly ran from the room
and quietly shut the door.

Just then he heard his mother call,
"Where are you, Benjamin?"
Running down the stairs, he knew
Jesus would be *his* Friend.

DEAR PARENT:

A rereading of the story of the Last Supper brings to the minds of most readers the painting by Leonardo da Vinci on the wall of the Convent of Santa Maria delle Grazie. In the fresco, a classical example of Renaissance design, all focuses on Christ. The vanishing point in the perspective of the picture is in the face of Christ. The mood is set. Christ would be alone in His suffering: No one would stand by Him or be ready to die with Him. We read of His last words and know how His life will end.

Yet the story of the Last Supper is prefaced in John 13:1 with these words: "Jesus . . . having loved His own who were in the world, He loved them to the end (RSV). Nothing is so constant as Christ's love and faithfulness. We read of the foot washing, of Judas' betrayal, of Christ's agony to pay for the sins of all mankind. But still through all Christ's love persists.

Explain to your child the meaning and history of God's covenant. Tell him often of the love of Christ, and try to teach, by word and example, the lifestyle of Christian love.

THE EDITOR

GOOD FRIDAY

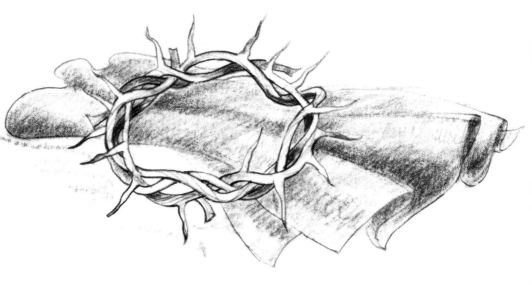

Matthew 21:1–27:61
Mark 11:1–15:47
Luke 19:28–23:56
John 12:12–19:42 for children
Written by Louise Ulmer
Illustrated by Reg Sandland

It was a bad day, a terrible day,
A day to run and hide.
So why do we say "Good Friday"
When we speak of the day Jesus died?

Though it seemed to be a hopeless day
When Jesus laid down His life,
It was part of the plan God had for His world
To make all the wrong things right.

The story began on Palm Sunday,
When Jesus rode into town.
"Hosanna to the king!" shouted followers,
As they spread green palm leaves down.

But Jesus had powerful enemies,
And His words often made them mad.
They decided to get even
By saying that Jesus was bad.

Over and over Jesus explained
That He wanted no throne or crown.
But His enemies said He planned to be king
And bring the government down.

When Jesus went to God's temple,
He saw merchants charging prices unfair.
"Get out," He said to the money changers,
"For this is a place of prayer."

Thursday, in the cool of the night,
When most of His friends were at home,
Jesus took His disciples to a garden.
They slept while He prayed alone.

Men marched to the garden with clubs and swords
While He told His disciples to pray.
When the crowd took Jesus to the high priest,
His disciples ran away.

The high priest sent Jesus to Pilate
On Friday before the first light.
God would give the life of His Son
To make all the wrong things right.

Angry men made fun of Jesus.
A soldier made Him a thorny crown.
His enemies gave Him a purple robe.
Others hit Him and pushed Him down.

"Behold your king," Governor Pilate cried.
"I'll punish Him and send Him home."
"We have no king but Caesar," the chief priests lied,
For those men had hearts of stone.

"Kill Him! Crucify Jesus!"
Shouted voices hateful and loud.
Pilate washed his hands of the problem
And gave in to the angry crowd.

As more of the people woke in the city,
They hurried to see what was done.
For Jesus the trials were over,
But the worst was yet to come.

Soldiers nailed Him to a cross,
Then planted it in the ground.
"Save yourself!" laughed His enemies.
But Jesus answered them not a sound.

As Jesus hung upon the cross
He knew His work was almost through.
He prayed to His heavenly Father,
"Forgive them; they know not what they do."

Near Jesus' cross stood Mary
And John, the disciple He loved.
"Here is your mother," He said to John.
"And, woman, here is your son."

The Son of God was dying.
Darkness covered the sun.
Jesus gave up His spirit and breathed His last;
His work on earth was done.

But though Jesus died and was buried,
The world had a great surprise.
For in three days, just as He promised,
Jesus would awaken and rise.

So you see, it was a sad day
When Jesus laid down His life.
But God raised Him to life again
To make all our wrong things right.

Dear Parents:

It is natural for your child to wonder why we call the day Jesus died "good." Your child may also wonder why anyone would want to kill Jesus—our best friend and helper. Explain to your child that we deserve to be punished for our sins, the bad things that we do. But because God loves us so much, He sent His only Son to die in our stead (John 3:16). God worked through the events of history, including the jealousy and fear of some religious leaders, to carry out His plan.

God's good plan rescued us from eternal death in hell. As Jesus died, He cried, "It is finished" (John 19:30). His redeeming work on earth was completed and He died as a victor.

Help your child understand the "good" in Good Friday—the goodness of a loving God who gives His children the gift of eternal life through the death and resurrection of His Son.

The Editor

Happy Easter

Matthew 27:57–28:10 for Children

Written by Gloria A. Truitt
Illustrated by Len Ebert

When Jesus died upon the cross,
    His friends looked on and cried;
For they had lost their Master,
    Their Lord and loving Guide.

A friend wrapped Jesus' body in
Fine linens; then he laid
Our Lord within his family tomb—
A cave that he had made.

To make sure no one could go in,
He rolled a giant stone
Across the entrance; then he left.
Now Jesus was alone.

While Jesus suffered on the cross,
    Two women watched nearby.
They both were grieving for their Lord,
    And, oh, how they did cry.

Both women were called Mary, and
    They loved the Lord, you see.
So, two days later they were filled
    With curiosity.

Toward the tomb they rushed with speed.
They had to take a look!
All at once an earthquake struck!
Imagine how they shook!

Then suddenly God's angel came
And rolled the stone away!
"Don't be afraid," the angel said.
"Come see where Jesus lay."

"Jesus is no longer here.
       He's risen from the dead!
Now, quickly go to Galilee
       And spread this news!" he said.

Before they left, the women looked
       Where Jesus had been placed.
Then overjoyed they said, "Let's run!
       There is no time to waste!"

So the women hurried off—
       Their hearts were filled with gladness!
"It must be true! He lives again!"
       No longer they felt sadness.

Then suddenly the women met
Their Savior on the way!
"Greetings!" Jesus said to them
On that first Easter day.

The women ran to Him and knelt
　　Before Him on the ground;
Then clasped His feet and worshiped Him—
　　Their Savior had been found!

Jesus said, "Don't be afraid!
Now go to Galilee
And tell My faithful followers
That there they will see Me!"

Purple stands for royalty,
 In case you didn't know,
Because the kings wore purple robes
 In days of long ago.

When Jesus was on trial that day—
 That day so sad and grim—
The folks who hated Jesus placed
 A purple robe on Him.

They yelled, "King of the Jews!" and laughed
 While making cruel fun.
How sad they didn't recognize
 Our Savior as God's Son.

The color white means clean and pure.
　　That's what the angel wore
When he rolled away the stone
　　That blocked the Lord's tomb door!

The joyous time of Easter comes
    Always during the spring
When, following the winter's chill,
    We hear the robins sing.

Now everywhere we look it seems
    That fresh, new life is seen—
From budding trees to crawly worms,
    And many sprouts of green.

Praise God for it is wonderful
    That Jesus came to earth,
Then died, but rose to live again,
    So *we* could have new birth!

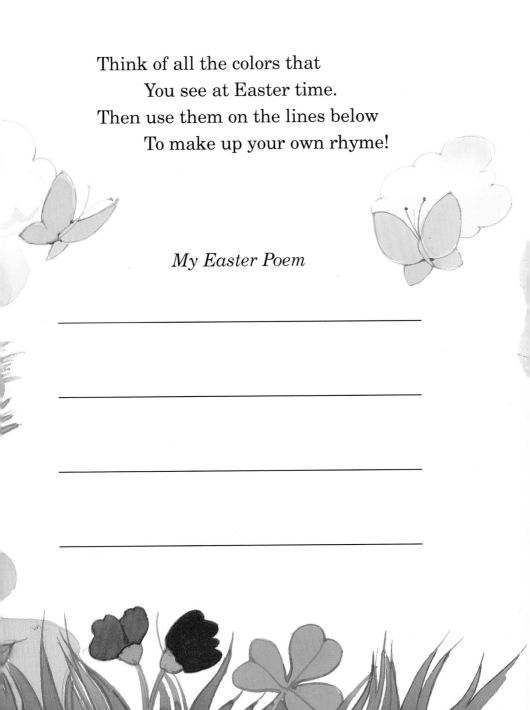

Think of all the colors that
 You see at Easter time.
Then use them on the lines below
 To make up your own rhyme!

My Easter Poem

_____

_____

_____

_____

God sacrificed His only Son
To save us from our sin;
And so *we* have eternal life,
Since we believe in Him!

My Easter Prayer